Living a Colourful LIFE

L. VALENTINE

To order additional copies of this book, contact:
Xlibris
1-800-455-039
www.xlibris.com.au
Orders@Xlibris.com.au

I can honestly say that this book is not all about my bad photography skills and above-average poetry.

As you read on, you might become confused and want to confirm if what you read is the truth.

Yes, it is. Or is it?

Continue if you dare …

My love of the beauty I experience through my eyes, combined with words, has inspired me to write. As indecisive as I am, I thought to shove my shyness out the window and turn my creativity into a book. This makes me laugh to myself, yet I wonder if other people in this world might enjoy my work as I do.

On a side note, my psychologist advised that I find a hobby that does not require other people to make me happy, since I was destroying my own life in the process of being a self-sacrificing helper.

So here we are today. You are reading my book, which conveys the places I have travelled to and the ideas and thoughts that appeared along the way, and I am thankful that I have successfully achieved something at least once in my life.

I do apologise in advance for my own selfishness in sharing my creativity with the world. But I remain the optimistic child who wants to see things through an innocent light. Who wants to read a story about someone being a martyr in his or her current life? Like, seriously!

Now, let's move on to something more interesting.

To make a Wish is to only Dream

But to Experience it,

Then it becomes your Reality.

I took this picture on my first cruise-ship holiday, which I went on with a childhood friend of more than twenty-four years. I took the picture as we were floating out of Sydney Harbour in Australia. The words were a lightning bolt to my brain when I first saw them through a flower-shop window years ago while riding a bus to work. I thought the moment was appropriate.

Of course, please interpret this image however you like. I could have printed it onto a huge canvas, then hung it on a wall as a conversation piece … No, too lazy.

Beauty is in the eye of the beholder

I took this photo as I admired the inner structure of a small historical church. At the time, I was on a package-arranged holiday tour with a work friend. We visited Wellington, New Zealand. It was her first time to the country, and we both absolutely loved it. I used to live there years ago, but it felt like my first visit to the city. We both wanted to stay longer.

Do you see what I see—the lighting, the architecture, and the colours combined? I thought it was all beautiful.

Now, we can agree to disagree. I have been to Rome, Italy, and entered the Vatican. And you're right that nothing can compare to those. But compared to locations of the legends of old, including the period of Robin Hood of Sherwood Forest in Nottingham, England—a real person and a real place that I was able to visit years ago—it's well preserved.

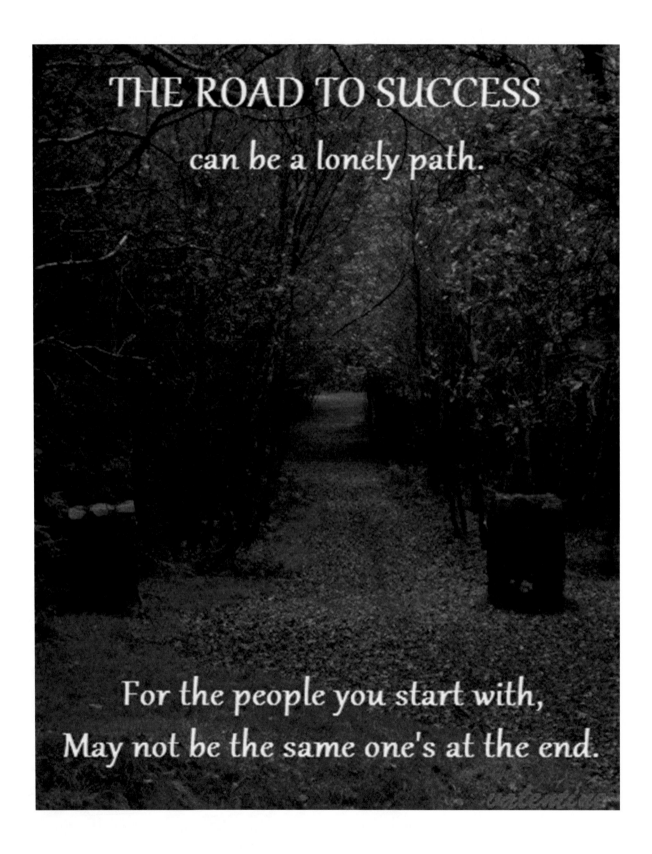

THE ROAD TO SUCCESS

can be a lonely path.

For the people you start with,
May not be the same one's at the end.

Travelling through the Irish countryside, I found that Dublin reminds me of home. I have called New Zealand home since the age of two. And here's just a little secret: the natural rocks in Dublin actually sparkle. It made me think that the leprechauns were real.

I don't think you can get away with it now, but back then, I collected small stones from every country I went to. I even took one from the Colosseum in Rome. Of course, we will keep that between just you and me. A friend was also kind enough to think about me as she sat on a stone, which she picked out of her butt crack. It belonged in a wall of a Swedish palace that she toured, and she brought it back for my collection. She was a really good friend.

Anyway, I went on this trip to Ireland on my own during a long weekend. I lost five kilograms in three to four days, which wasn't healthy when I now think about it. But when I was unsure about when the next toilet stop would come, I refused to eat or drink anything other than the bare minimum.

When I saw the view shown in this photo, my mind ran a mile a minute regarding how to be creative with the image. This is the result. *Appropriate, as a lone traveller.*

A Gentle Kiss from the Sun,

A light Touch of the Wind.

It is only you who I wait for,

And forever will I Adore.

Australian summers can be intensely hot. I took this photo the summer of the year of the Ice Bucket Challenge. In New Zealand and Australia, the challenge raised money for cancer. In the United States, it raised money for a different charity.

Also, that year, I saved an orange tree in my backyard, and I took a photo of newly grown leaves soaking up the sun. It created a thought-provoking visual, and this photo is the result. I'll never do the Ice Bucket Challenge again.

I chose participants for the challenge, a video of which I've posted on YouTube, who were John Key (the New Zealand prime minister), Ian Somerhalder (the American TV star), Julie Cesar (the British TV presenter), and my ex-boss from when I lived in London. They also included my travel friend Kendra from Canada and my ex-workmate Steve, who was a gym junkie and for a short stint my personal trainer.

Why? Because I'm unique.

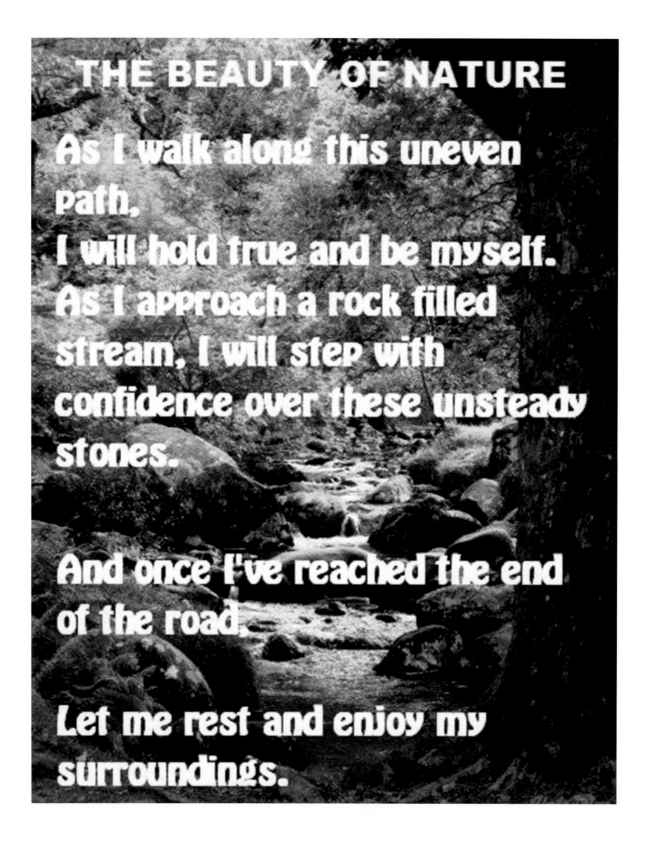

THE BEAUTY OF NATURE

As I walk along this uneven path,
I will hold true and be myself.
As I approach a rock filled stream, I will step with confidence over these unsteady stones.

And once I've reached the end of the road,

Let me rest and enjoy my surroundings.

This is another nature shot from the Irish countryside outside Dublin. I took it not far from the fields where *Braveheart* was filmed, with Mel Gibson shouting, "Freedom!" before he gets executed and slashed into pieces. It is a gruesome film that I only vaguely remember watching. I think I was too young for the movie when it came out, so my parents restricted me from watching the entire movie. I shrug my shoulders now, remembering I only liked his *Mad Max* films. Weren't those more gruesome?

No, my parents didn't think so.

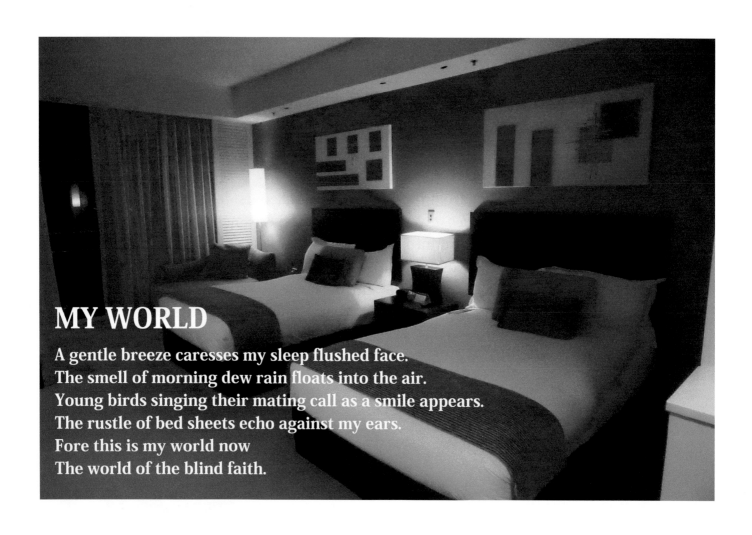

MY WORLD

A gentle breeze caresses my sleep flushed face.
The smell of morning dew rain floats into the air.
Young birds singing their mating call as a smile appears.
The rustle of bed sheets echo against my ears.
Fore this is my world now
The world of the blind faith.

A hurricane was hitting the Gold Coast of Australia at the time I took this picture. I took it the night my long-time childhood friend Sam and I were supposed to fly back home after an all-girls weekend of fun.

Who would have guessed that not only would our flight get cancelled due to "tech problems," but the airline would be awesome enough to charter us a private bus to go stay in a five-star resort for the night, provide us with a fifty-dollar credit, and rebook us a morning flight at no charge? Now, how amazing is that?

This photo shows our hotel room. There, we ordered a lot of food and drinks and made friends with other passengers as we gathered in our room to party the night away. We nearly missed our bus transfer back to the airport, but it was all worth the experience.

After arriving at the airport, Sam and I caught up with our other friends who we met up with at the weekend convention and who were using the same airline. The previous day, when they had received notice of a possible cancellation, they decided to pay extra money to book another flight for the next day. One poor guy hadn't had the ability to extend his luxury accommodation, but another good friend let him crash on the floor of his two-star hotel room. So he was the worse for wear that morning, and his eyes showed his devastation when we told him that if he had actually showed up at the airport, he would have gotten the same benefit we got. I'm sure you can imagine his reaction.

You can't blame me, though. I had thought about him for two seconds, deciding whether I should call him. I had posted it to my fellow travellers on all the Facebook chat groups. I didn't realise that he was not part of the chats. But he had seemed in capable hands while enjoying himself before we left. So I didn't call.

EXPERIENCE LOVE

Love is to be experienced.
Love has no regrets.
It may sometimes hurt,
And can even feel obsessive.
But the power of love,
Can be a beautiful thing.

Once a year, for a few weeks, Sydney holds a special event called Sculpture by the Sea. Various artists display their work along the coast of Bondi Beach. The day I attended, I took heaps of pictures, of course, but I must say that the structure in this photo was one of my favourites that day.

I think this is an appropriate poem to accompany the photo, but it's a shame that when I wrote this, I had tried out Internet dating, encouraged by a friend who is a serial online dater. I tried a military website and thought I'd meet someone I could really connect with. While I exchanged pictures and messaged with a guy, I grew quite attached.

One day, the guy's friend messaged me and sent photos showing that the guy had gotten ambushed and been in a serious accident. Apparently, that was why he hadn't contacted me for a few days, and I wasn't supposed to know about the accident. His friend let me know what had happened in secret.

Hearing the guy was alive but had a head injury left me severely traumatised. Like a normal person, I couldn't think straight at the time. I just knew that I wanted to see him, talk to him, and do anything, really. I felt a sense of desperation that I'd never felt before. It made me think that he was the one for me and that was it. No one else mattered. He had proposed to me before the communication stopped. I felt hesitant at the time, but now, after the accident, if I heard him ask me to marry him—if he just opened his eyes and sent a picture showing him happily smiling—then I knew I'd 100 per cent say yes.

It started with one hundred dollars for communication fees. A week or two later, I sent him another six hundred American dollars. After a month, he was awake. I was so happy. Then, he said he'd decided to quit the special forces and come live with me. But he needed help getting out of service, with fees and charges involved.

They say that love is blind, and I can truly say that I was.

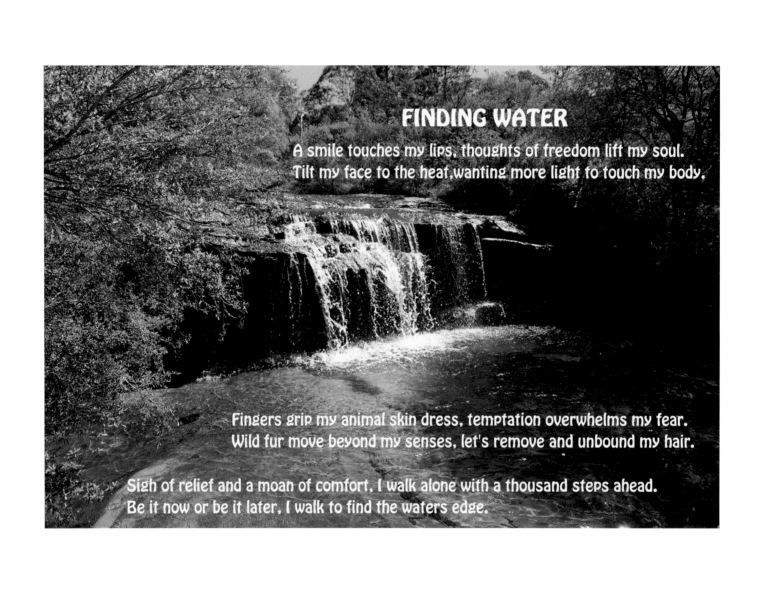

FINDING WATER

A smile touches my lips, thoughts of freedom lift my soul.
Tilt my face to the heat, wanting more light to touch my body.

Fingers grip my animal skin dress, temptation overwhelms my fear.
Wild fur move beyond my senses, let's remove and unbound my hair.

Sigh of relief and a moan of comfort, I walk alone with a thousand steps ahead.
Be it now or be it later, I walk to find the waters edge.

This poem is unique to me because as part of a poetry society, I like to participate in competitions to win awards and recognition. This one contest required X-rated writing, and I thought I would give it a go. It involved a picture of a naked female walking through a field while wearing a small fur vest that hid nothing. Only her back faced us, and I'll leave the rest to your imagination. My feedback stated that the poem I wrote wasn't erotically descriptive enough. I guess my mind is just not dirty enough.

This picture I've combined the poem with was during a four-hour hike with my dad in the Blue Mountains of Australia. On that hike, we looked at various waterfalls and took great pictures of nature. And we searched for a native lizard that was promoted on the signboards we passed. It really surprised him how durably and fast I could walk for an overweight young lady who generally didn't do a lot of exercise and was a couch potato. He also impressed me, considering he was an old man and not a spring chicken anymore. I secretly hoped that he didn't collapse along the track, as I wondered how I would carry him back home.

Poor dad was traumatised during our walk. While I took some pictures of rock caves next to a river, he went exploring and found a toilet-dumping site. As he expressed his displeasure, I wondered, *Could it have been the old man and dog from earlier? The two older ladies carrying backpacks? The young lady who had power-walked past us earlier?*

I reckon it was one of the two old ladies, but who knows for sure …

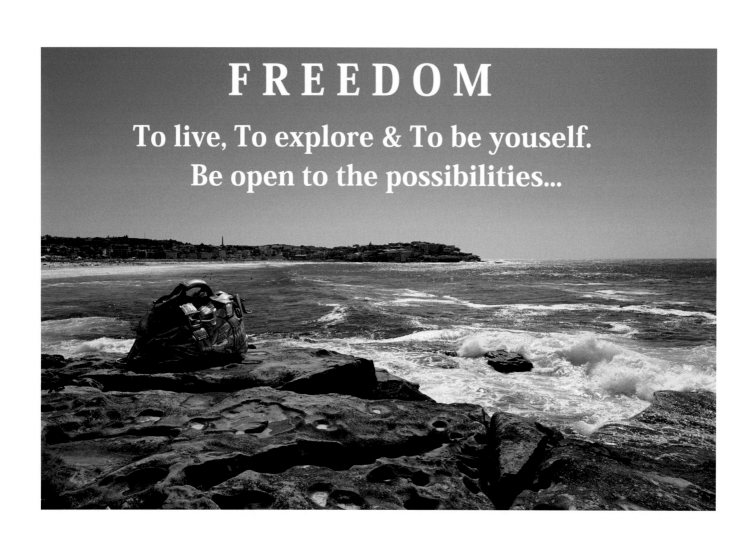

FREEDOM

To live, To explore & To be youself.
Be open to the possibilities...

This photo's scene is from the Sydney event Sculpture by the Sea; that is Bondi Beach in the background.

Free will or freedom of expression—it might hold true, but that doesn't mean that free expression should always be done. And yet, here I am, about to contradict myself.

Out of high school, I had a career as a makeup artist for film and television. And I was good at my job. I started to become well known and in demand. But I gave it all up when I decided to move away from home to another city.

Next, I went overseas to London for nearly two years. I made heaps of money, travelled through Europe, and got to try cocaine—just a taste. I joined a vampire society group and wore gothic clothes, gained another tattoo, and went on cemetery visits and ghost tours for fun. I even got custom-made vamp teeth and a *Matrix*-style ankle-length leather jacket that I pull out during Halloween when I have the chance.

For the first two years of my life in Sydney, I joined a BDSM secret society group, which gained me private entry into a world 100 per cent more erotic than *Fifty Shades of Grey*.

I was also in a threesome relationship of a one-man, two-women combo. The relationship ended when he became suicidal, and she was already depressed. They were kind enough to not have me involved during their destructive episodes. The last thing I saw on Facebook, they are still together. But he's now a woman.

As I see life, have no regrets. Play safe. Try everything at least once, within reason.

STILL TOGETHER

You know that you've lived well, When the one you love is still beside you.

Each night you go to bed, And every morning you wake up.
Still able to look in each others eyes, And say the words "I love you"

If one day I turn around and find you not there, I'll just close my eye and follow behind you.

I titled this poem "Still Together" because I think the goal of any human being is to find someone he or she can grow old with—a companion for life. That's what I believe.

When people are young, they all have dreams of their future careers and who they will become. And everyone hears the usual: "I want to be a doctor when I grow up." "I'm going to be a police officer." The list goes on.

Now, I don't know if you'd call it *brainwashing*, but my favourite books were *Cinderella*, *Sleeping Beauty*, *Snow White*, and *The Little Mermaid*. So, of course, growing up, I said my goal was to marry my handsome prince and live happily ever after.

I was five years old at the time—a cute age. I had my first kiss under the red grape tree in the backyard that year. My neighbour's older sister instructed him and me on how it should be done. We got on quite well, until his sister told all the kids at school about it. Of course, I wouldn't accept the outcome.

My angry reply was "She kissed him too!" I mean, how else were we supposed to know how to kiss?

TROPICAL DESIRE

Thoroughly soak in the juices of coconut milk.

Apply crushed mango, pawpaw and oranges like a face mask.

Deeply massage your hair, hands and feet with flower scented oils.

Rinse yourself under the crisp fresh waterfalls or

dive into the crystal clear sea.

Feel the blazing heat of the tropical sun as you lay naked and bare.

Hear the tinkling of sea shells as they move to the sea breeze.

Once you are ready, prepare for the touch of coconut oil lathered hands.

To spread the amazing passion with only you

and your tropical desire.

This image shows my first poem that won me an award. The poem received many likes and comments, and it was also recommended for publishing. I accepted the offer and had it printed in a poetry anthology with many other writers' work.

I ONLY SEE YOU

Plump soft lips,
Eyes dazzle hypnotically.

Hair shiney and smooth,
Pink flushed cheeks.

Attention only for you.

I took this photo in the Botanic Garden of Wellington City. I wrote the poem for a competition that had guidelines to write a poem with as few words as you can. Of course, I didn't come anywhere. But I did garner a lot of comments and likes, some wishing that the poem was longer, et cetera …

If they only knew.

Would you believe me if I told you that I don't like kids? I think they are cute and adorable as babies, because you can hand them back to the parents when they start crying, puke, or dirty their nappies.

Also, newborn babies are scary. If you've never held one before, then you won't understand. I have anxiety I will squish them to death by holding them too tight, or maybe drop them, which will give them brain damage, ruining their lives forever! Oh, and when they get sick? I try not to kill them with a drug overdose. All these thoughts continuously run through my head. And if they aren't potty-trained and self-sufficient, don't even think of me babysitting. My sister calls me the "mean auntie" who will wack babies' behinds or isolate them in another room if they misbehave or start crying.

The point is I wrote this poem to describe human babies. They are so edible and soft like marshmallows, especially when they have just woken up.

Follow a Successful Leader who has already built a bridge that you also want to walk on. The path is already there, you just need to follow it.

I was in Melbourne, Australia, for the very first time when I toured the harbour and took this picture. I went there for a weekend business-training convention. There, I hung out with great friends and was introduced to some great people as well. When you can mix and mingle with millionaires living the life of their dreams, they tell you the secrets to their success. How could that not put a sparkle in my eyes? The training system taught at the convention is proven, as it pumps out multimillionaires every year. Lucky! Well, not really. They deserve their successes, and I congratulate those who have travelled the road before me.

ADVENTUROUS HISTORY

DESCENDANTS OF A ROYAL POLYNESIAN KING
IT'S MY DUTY TO LEARN OF MY PRIVILEGED UPBRINGING.

FROM FRENCH/GERMAN MISSIONARIES WHO EXPLORED THE VAST WORLD.

TO DARK AFRICAN SLAVES WHO TRAVELED AS MAIDSERVANTS.

FAST FORWARD A FEW YEARS TO CHINESE WAR FIGHTERS, ALONG SIDE GAINT
WARRIOR HUNTERS WHICH CAPTAIN COOK NAMED FROM "SAVAGE ISLAND"

THROUGH THE AGES OF TIME AND THE ADVENTUROUS HISTORY I'VE GAINED,
IT'S NO SURPRISE TO BELIEVE I TOO EXPLORE AND DO THE SAME.

I also took this photo at the Wellington Botanic Garden in Wellington City, New Zealand. I gained an award for this poem. The poetry contest asked for poems that explain who you are, but this poems tells my family history in a nutshell. The only discrepancy involves my mother's relative, who I believed was an African maidservant but was really a gardener. My sister and I argued over this until she was proven correct.

Also, in my father's family, the male descendants had a history of renaming their bloodlines after their own first names. This stopped at my father's generation. As you would guess, this created confusion on the tropical island the family came from, because as time went on, you wouldn't know whether the person you were dating was a relative. And incest is very bad. So, there is an unspoken law within our culture that if you find the person you are interested in comes from the same tropical island or is a descendant of the same island, you must confirm the identity of his or her grandparents, aunties, and uncles.

If you confirm you are related, an immediate break-up should occur, or no attempt at further flirtation. But I'll tell you a secret …

There's a rumour in my family that I might or might not have a relative born from such a close union.

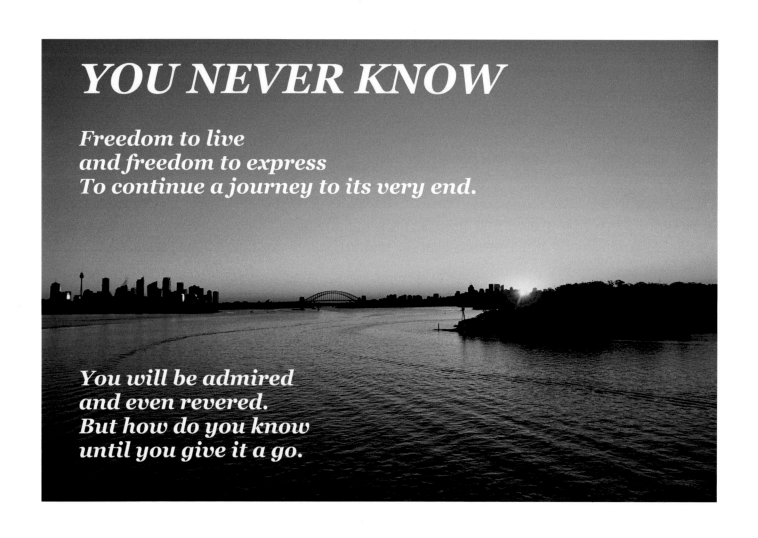

YOU NEVER KNOW

Freedom to live
and freedom to express
To continue a journey to its very end.

You will be admired
and even revered.
But how do you know
until you give it a go.

As I started with my cruise-ship-experience picture, I thought I'd end my book with the same. Again, I took this leaving Sydney Harbour to go on a great adventure.

This is not the entire poem, but it's a quote from one of my favourite movies featuring Tom Hanks. I'll change it up a little and just say, "Life can be like a box of chocolates, because you never know which to choose and what you are going to get inside."

I hope you have enjoyed the journey of how I see the world and all the different adventures that I've had, or you have found your own meaning in my poetry. Did you find reading this book as entertaining as I found writing it?

Thank you for reading.

Printed in the United States
By Bookmasters